Financial Literacy for All

A Guide to Managing Money and Building Wealth

I. Introduction

- Definition of financial literacy
- Importance of financial literacy

II. Basic Money Management

- Budgeting
- Saving and managing debt
- Understanding credit scores and credit reports

III. Investing

- Types of investments
- Risk management
- Building a diversified portfolio

IV. Building Wealth

- Building an emergency fund
- Long-term savings and retirement planning
- Real estate investing

V. Tax Planning and Insurance

- Understanding taxes
- Tax planning strategies
- Types of insurance and how to choose the right coverage

VI. Special Considerations

- Managing finances as a single person
- Money management for families
- Finances for small business owners

VII. Conclusion

- Recap of key takeaways

INTRODUCTION

"Financial Literacy for All: A Guide to Managing Money and Building Wealth" is designed to provide a comprehensive guide to managing money and building wealth for all individuals. Financial literacy is the ability to understand and manage one's finances effectively. It is an essential skill that is often overlooked, yet it plays a crucial role in achieving financial stability and independence. The purpose of this book is to empower readers with the knowledge and skills they need to take control of their finances and build a secure financial future.

The book will cover a wide range of topics, from basic money management and budgeting to investing and building wealth. It will also delve into special considerations such as managing finances as a single person, money management for families, and finances for small business owners. The book will be easy to understand and will be aimed at readers of all levels of financial knowledge.

This guide will provide readers with the tools they need to make informed financial decisions, reduce debt, save for the future and reach their financial goals. Whether you are just starting out and looking to build a solid foundation for your financial future, or you are an experienced investor looking to take your wealth-building efforts to the next level, "Financial Literacy for All" is the perfect guide for you.

We will explore the different types of investments, the risk management, and how to build a diversified portfolio. We will also delve into tax planning and insurance, providing readers with the information they need to make informed decisions about taxes and insurance coverage. The book will be filled with practical tips, real-life examples and the latest research on personal finance. With this guide, readers will be equipped with the knowledge and skills they need to make smart financial decisions and build a secure financial future.

DEFINITION OF FINANCIAL LITERACY

Financial literacy is the ability to understand and manage one's finances effectively. It includes a range of knowledge and skills, such as budgeting, saving, investing, and understanding taxes and insurance. Financial literacy is essential for achieving financial stability and independence, as it enables individuals to make informed financial decisions and reach their financial goals.

Financial literacy is not just about understanding financial concepts, but also about applying that knowledge in real-life situations. It involves being able to evaluate financial products and services, understand the terms and conditions, and make informed decisions about spending, saving and investing.

Financial literacy is a lifelong process, and it is essential to continue to learn and adapt as the financial landscape changes. This means keeping up with new financial products, understanding changes in tax laws, and staying informed about new trends in the economy.

Financial literacy is important for people of all ages and income levels. Whether you are just starting out, looking to build a solid foundation for your financial future, or you are an experienced investor looking to take your wealth-building efforts to the next level, financial literacy is an essential skill that will help you make informed financial decisions and reach your financial goals.

In this book, we will explore the different aspects of financial literacy, providing readers with the knowledge and skills they need to make informed financial decisions and build a secure financial future. We will cover a wide range of topics, from basic money management and budgeting to investing and building wealth, as well as special considerations such as managing finances as a single person, money management for families, and finances for small business owners.

IMPORTANCE OF FINANCIAL LITERACY

1. Achieving financial stability and independence: Financial literacy enables individuals to make informed financial decisions and reach their financial goals, which is crucial for achieving financial stability and independence. This includes understanding how to budget, save, invest, and manage debt, as well as understanding taxes and insurance.

2. Making informed financial decisions: Financial literacy enables individuals to evaluate financial products and services, understand the terms and conditions, and make informed decisions about spending, saving and investing. This can help individuals avoid financial scams and predatory lending practices, and can also help them make the most of their money.

3. Planning for the future: Financial literacy is essential for long-term financial planning,

such as saving for retirement, building an emergency fund, and planning for unexpected expenses. It allows individuals to make informed decisions about their financial future and take control of their financial lives.

4. Reducing stress and anxiety: Financial literacy can help individuals feel more in control of their finances and reduce stress and anxiety related to money. This can improve overall well-being and quality of life.

5. Improving credit scores: Financial literacy helps individuals understand how credit scores are determined and how to improve them. This can open up more opportunities for borrowing and make it easier to qualify for loans and credit cards with better terms and lower interest rates.

6. **Building wealth:** Financial literacy is essential for building wealth over time. It allows individuals to make informed investment decisions, understand the risks and rewards of different investments, and build a diversified portfolio.

7. **Empowerment**: Financial literacy empowers individuals to take control of their financial lives and make decisions that align with their goals and values. It helps people to understand the importance of their role in managing their own money, and how to use it to their advantage.

8. **Improving financial knowledge:** Financial literacy is a lifelong process and it is essential to continue to learn and adapt as the financial landscape changes. This means keeping up with new financial products, understanding changes in tax laws, and staying informed about new trends in the economy.

9. **Encouraging entrepreneurship:**
Financial literacy can help individuals understand the basics of starting and running a business, such as creating a budget, managing cash flow and financial record keeping. This knowledge can help individuals start and grow their own business, which can lead to job creation and economic growth.

10. **Promoting social mobility:** Financial literacy can help individuals from disadvantaged backgrounds to understand the importance of managing money and investing for the future, which can promote social mobility and help to reduce income inequality. Additionally, it can help individuals from disadvantaged backgrounds to understand and navigate the financial systems and products that are available to them.

PURPOSE OF THE BOOK

The purpose of "Financial Literacy for All: A Guide to Managing Money and Building Wealth" is to provide a comprehensive guide to managing money and building wealth for all individuals. The book is designed to be easy to understand and accessible to readers of all levels of financial knowledge.

The book will cover a wide range of topics, including basic money management and budgeting, saving and managing debt, understanding credit scores and credit reports, types of investments, risk management and building a diversified portfolio, building an emergency fund, long-term savings and retirement planning, real estate investing, tax planning, and insurance.

The book will also delve into special considerations such as managing finances as a single person, money management for families, and finances for small business owners. This will provide readers with a comprehensive understanding of the different financial challenges and considerations that different individuals may face.

This guide is intended to be an essential resource for individuals of all ages and income levels who want to take control of their finances, reduce debt, save for the future and reach their financial goals. Whether you are just starting out, looking to build a solid foundation for your financial future, or you are an experienced investor looking to take your wealth-building efforts to the next level, this guide is for you.

BASIC MONEY MANAGEMENT

Basic money management is the foundation of financial literacy. It involves understanding how to budget, save, and manage debt. This section of the book will cover these basic concepts and provide readers with the tools they need to take control of their finances and build a solid foundation for their financial future.

1. **Budgeting**

   Budgeting is the process of creating a plan for how to spend and save money. It involves setting financial goals and creating a spending plan that aligns with those goals. A budget can help individuals stay on track with their finances, ensure that they have enough money to cover their expenses, and plan for future expenses.

   Creating a budget begins with identifying all of your income sources, including your salary, any rental income, or any other sources of income. Then, you will list all of your expenses, including fixed expenses such as rent or mortgage payments, and variable expenses such as groceries and entertainment. Subtracting your total expenses from your total income will give you an idea of how much money you have left over.

A budget can be created in different ways, such as using a spreadsheet, a budgeting app, or a pen and paper. The important thing is to find a method that works for you, and that you can stick to. There are also different budgeting methods, such as the zero-sum budget, which involves allocating every dollar of your income to a specific category, or the 50/30/20 rule, which allocates 50% of your income to essential expenses, 30% to discretionary expenses, and 20% to savings and debt repayment.

Budgeting can help individuals to identify areas where they may be overspending, and make adjustments accordingly. It can also help to prioritize expenses and ensure that money is being spent on things that are truly important.

2. Saving

Saving is another important aspect of basic money management. It involves setting aside money for future expenses or goals. Saving can help individuals build an emergency fund, which can provide a safety net in case of unexpected expenses. It also helps individuals to save for long-term goals, such as retirement or buying a house.

Creating a saving plan is similar to creating a budget, it begins with setting a savings goal, and then determining how much money needs to be set aside each month to reach that goal. There are different types of savings accounts, such as a traditional savings account, a certificate of deposit, or a money market account. Each of these accounts has different features, such as interest rates, minimum balance requirements, and withdrawal restrictions, so it's important to choose the right one based on your individual needs.

3. **Managing debt**

   Managing debt is another essential aspect of basic money management. It involves understanding how to borrow money and how to repay it. The most important thing is to avoid taking on too much debt, and to make sure that any debt that is taken on is manageable. This means understanding the terms and conditions of any loan, including the interest rate, the repayment period, and any fees.

   Managing debt also involves creating a plan to repay any outstanding debts. This can be done by creating a debt repayment plan, which involves listing all of your debts, the interest rate, and the minimum monthly payment. You can then prioritize the debts that you want to repay first, and allocate money each month to repay them. There are also debt management strategies like the snowball method and the avalanche method, which can help you to manage and pay off your debts more efficiently.

In summary, basic money management is a crucial part of financial literacy that involves understanding how to budget, save and manage debt effectively. By creating a budget, saving plan, and debt management plan, individuals can take control of their finances, reduce debt, save for the future and reach their financial goals.

INVESTING

Investing is an important aspect of money management that can help individuals to grow their wealth over time. Investing involves putting money into assets such as stocks, bonds, real estate, or mutual funds, with the expectation that these assets will increase in value.

TYPES OF INVESTMENTS

There are many different types of investments, each with its own set of risks and rewards. Some of the most common types of investments include:

1. **Stocks:** A stock represents a small ownership share in a company. When a company makes a profit, the value of the stock may increase, and the stockholder may earn money through dividends or by selling the stock at a higher price. However, the value of a stock can also decrease if the company performs poorly.

2. **Bonds:** A bond is a loan that is made to a company or government. When an investor buys a bond, they are effectively lending money to the issuer. In return, the issuer promises to pay interest and return the original investment at maturity.

3. **Real estate:** Real estate investments involve buying property with the expectation that the value of the property will increase over time. This can be done through the purchase of a rental property, or through the purchase of real estate investment trusts (REITs), which allow individuals to invest in real estate without actually buying property.

4. **Mutual Funds:** A mutual fund is a type of investment that pools money from many investors to buy a diversified portfolio of stocks, bonds, and other securities. This allows individuals to invest in a variety of assets with a smaller amount of money.

RISK MANAGEMENT

Investing involves taking on risk, but it is important to understand and manage that risk. One of the most effective ways to manage risk is through diversification, which involves spreading your investments across different types of assets, sectors, and geographic locations. This can help to reduce the risk of losing money if any one investment performs poorly.

BUILDING A DIVERSIFIED PORTFOLIO

Building a diversified portfolio is an important aspect of investing. It involves investing in a mix of different types of assets, such as stocks, bonds, and real estate, in order to spread out the risk. A diversified portfolio can help to reduce the overall risk of the portfolio, while still providing the opportunity for growth.

In summary, investing is an important aspect of money management that can help individuals to grow their wealth over time. There are many different types of investments, each with its own set of risks and rewards. Investing involves taking on risk, but it is important to understand and manage that risk through diversification and building a diversified portfolio. By investing in a mix of different types of assets, individuals can reduce the overall risk of their portfolio, while still providing the opportunity for growth.

BUILDING WEALTH

Building wealth is an important aspect of money management that involves creating a plan to grow one's financial assets over time. This section of the book will cover strategies for building wealth, including building an emergency fund, long-term savings and retirement planning, and real estate investing.

1. **Building an emergency fund:** An emergency fund is a savings account that is set aside to cover unexpected expenses, such as a job loss, medical emergency, or home repair. An emergency fund can provide a safety net in case of unexpected expenses, and can help individuals avoid going into debt when faced with an emergency. Building an emergency fund typically involves setting aside a specific amount of money each month, and keeping the funds in a savings account that is easily accessible. It is generally recommended to

have at least three to six months' worth of living expenses in an emergency fund.

2. **Long-term savings and retirement planning:** Long-term savings and retirement planning involve setting aside money for future expenses or goals, such as retirement. This can be done by creating a savings plan, which involves setting a savings goal and determining how much money needs to be set aside each month to reach that goal. Additionally, one can consider investing in retirement accounts such as 401(k)s or IRAs, which offer tax advantages and compound interest, to help grow retirement savings over time.

3. **Real estate investing:** Real estate investing involves buying property with the expectation that the value of the property will increase over time. This can be done through the purchase of a rental property,

or through the purchase of real estate investment trusts (REITs), which allow individuals to invest in real estate without actually buying property. Real estate investing can be a great way to build wealth over time, but it also carries risks and requires a significant amount of money upfront.

In summary, building wealth is an important aspect of money management that involves creating a plan to grow one's financial assets over time. Building an emergency fund, long-term savings and retirement planning, and real estate investing are all strategies that can help individuals to build wealth over time. However, it is important to remember that building wealth takes time and requires a commitment to saving and investing for the long-term.

TAX PLANNING AND INSURANCE

Tax planning and insurance are both important aspects of money management that can help individuals to save money and protect their assets. This section of the book will cover strategies for tax planning and insurance, including understanding tax laws, deductions and credits, and the different types of insurance.

Tax planning is the process of organizing your financial affairs in a way that minimizes your tax liability. This involves understanding the tax laws and regulations, and taking advantage of deductions and credits that are available. Tax planning can help individuals to save money on their taxes, and can also help to ensure that they are in compliance with tax laws.

Some of the most common tax deductions include charitable contributions, mortgage interest, and state and local taxes. Tax credits, on the other hand, are dollar-for-dollar reductions of the taxes you owe. Examples of credits include the Child Tax

Credit, the Earned Income Tax Credit, and the
American Opportunity Tax Credit.

 Insurance is a way to protect yourself and your
assets from financial loss. There are many
different types of insurance, each with its own set
of risks and benefits. Some of the most common
types of insurance include:

1. Health insurance: Health insurance helps to
    cover the cost of medical care, including
    doctor visits, prescription drugs, and
    hospital stays.

2. Auto insurance: Auto insurance provides
    coverage for accidents and damage to your
    vehicle, as well as liability coverage in case
    you are found to be at fault in an accident.

3. Homeowners insurance: Homeowners
    insurance provides coverage for damage to
    your home and personal property, as well

as liability coverage in case someone is injured on your property.

4. Life insurance: Life insurance provides a death benefit to your beneficiaries in the event of your death. This can help to ensure that your loved ones are financially protected in the event of your death.

It's important to understand the different types of insurance available and how they can benefit you. It's also important to review your insurance coverage regularly to ensure that it still meets your needs and that you are not overpaying for coverage that you don't need.

In summary, tax planning and insurance are both important aspects of money management that can help individuals to save money and protect their assets. Tax planning involves understanding the tax laws and regulations, and taking advantage of deductions and credits that are available. Insurance is a way to protect yourself and your assets from financial loss. It is important to understand the different types of insurance available, and review your coverage regularly to ensure that it still meets your needs.

SPECIAL CONSIDERATIONS

Money management can be different for different individuals, depending on their unique circumstances. This section of the book will cover special considerations for managing money, including managing finances as a single person, money management for families, and finances for small business owners.

MANAGING FINANCES AS A SINGLE

PERSON: Managing finances as a single person can have its own unique challenges. Single individuals may have to manage all of their finances on their own and may not have the support of a partner. This can make budgeting, saving, and investing more challenging. It's important for single individuals to take extra care to plan for the future, build an emergency fund, and have a clear understanding of their financial situation.

MONEY MANAGEMENT FOR FAMILIES:

Managing money as a family can also have its own set of challenges. Families may have to budget for multiple people, and may also have additional expenses such as child care and education. It's important for families to establish a budget that works for everyone, and to communicate regularly about their financial goals and plans. It's also important to teach children about money management and the value of saving.

FINANCES FOR SMALL BUSINESS OWNERS:

Managing finances as a small business owner can be complex, as business owners must balance the needs of their business with their personal finances. This can include managing cash flow, budgeting for business expenses, and understanding taxes and regulations. It's important for small business owners to have a clear understanding of their financial situation, and to create a financial plan that takes into account the unique needs of their business.

In summary, money management can be different for different individuals, depending on their unique circumstances. This section of the book covers special considerations for managing money, including managing finances as a single person, money management for families, and finances for small business owners. It's important for individuals to take into account their unique circumstances when planning and managing their finances.

CONCLUSION

In conclusion, "Financial Literacy for All: A Guide to Managing Money and Building Wealth" has aimed to provide a comprehensive guide to managing money and building wealth for all individuals. The book has covered a wide range of topics, including basic money management and budgeting, saving and managing debt, understanding credit scores and credit reports, types of investments, risk management and building a diversified portfolio, building an emergency fund, long-term savings and retirement planning, real estate investing, tax planning, and insurance.

It has also delved into special considerations such as managing finances as a single person, money management for families, and finances for small business owners. The goal of this book is to provide readers with the knowledge and skills they need to make informed financial decisions and build a secure financial future.

It's important to note that financial literacy is a continuous process, and one should always strive to improve their knowledge and understanding of personal finance. Remember that budgeting, saving, investing, tax planning, and insurance are all important aspects of money management that can help individuals to save money and protect their assets. With a solid understanding of these concepts, individuals can take control of their finances, reduce debt, save for the future and reach their financial goals.